Countryside
Dog Walks

Lake District - South

D1434530

Seddon Neudorfer

Publishing Ltd

www.countrysidedogwalks.co.uk

First published in February 2013 by **Wet Nose Publishing Ltd**,
Summer Roost
Graigfechan
Denbighshire
LL15 2EU

All enquiries regarding sales telephone: 01824 704398

email cdw@wetnosepublishing.co.uk

www.countrysidedogwalks.co.uk

ISBN 978-0-9573722-1-4

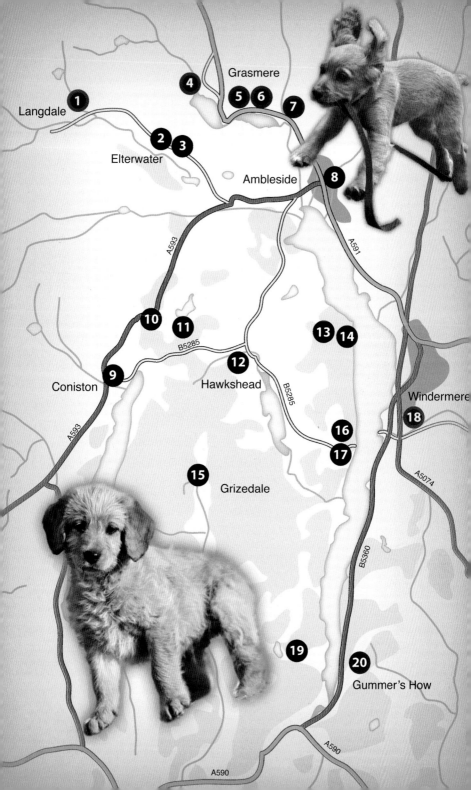

Langdale

1

4 Grasmere

5 6 7

2 3

Elterwater

Ambleside

8

A593

A591

10

11

B5285

13 14

12

9

Coniston

Hawkshead

B5285

Windermere

18

16

A593

17

15 Grizedale

A5074

B5360

19

20

Gummer's How

A590

A590

Contents

Introduction

The twenty walks included in this book are all designed so that you and your wet nosed friend have a really enjoyable time. There are a few specially designed stiles, which have lift gates for dogs. At a quick glance there is information at the beginning of each walk to tell you what to expect and what you may need to take with you. The descriptive guides will also warn of any roads ahead or areas of livestock so that you can get your dog on the lead well in advance.

Dogs just love to explore new places. They really enjoy the new smells and carry themselves a little higher with the added excitement. Going to new places gets you and your dog out and about meeting new people and their dogs. It is important to socialise dogs, as they will be more likely to act in a friendly manner towards other dogs as they gain confidence.

The stunning pictures in this book are just a taster of what you can see along the way. Most of the walks are crammed with fantastic views and you are never far from water or woodlands, the later will provide shade in the summer and shelter on cold, wet days where your dog will love the freedom to run up and down.

The walks are graded Easy, Medium and Challenging. They are all around one to three hours long, depending on you or your dog's pace. You may start with the easy ones and work up to the challenging walks depending on you and your dog's fitness. Different dog breeds and dog age must be taken into account when you decide which walks to do. If you are unsure of the distance that your dog can manage why not try the linear walks first. You will be able to judge if your dog is getting tired and so you can choose to turn back at any time. This is always good for older dogs, as some days are better than others and the linear walks are often flat making it easier to manage.

Different breeds of dog have different levels of fitness. For example Bull dogs can only do short walks where as a Border collie or a Springer spaniel are extremely agile and difficult to tire out. It is recommended that you research information on the breed of dog that you own to get to know what sort of exercise that they require.

You may have a walk that you are happy doing with your dog every day, but this book will show you new areas to explore with a change of scenery and a chance to meet new people and their dogs. Dogs love new places to visit and you will see the change in them as they explore the new surroundings, taking in the new smells with delight. You will fulfil your life and your dogs just by trying somewhere new.

The Grizedale and High Dam walks are mainly covered by trees where your dog can enjoy the freedom to run up and down without you having to worry about livestock. These walks are also great for hot days, as many dogs do not cope well in the sun.

There is plenty of water for your dog to enjoy, whether it be lakes, tarns or rivers, so for those dogs that love water you can be sure they won't stay dry for long.

Some of the walks include bridleways, so you may encounter horses. It is important to put your dog on a lead if you see horses approach. It is always helpful to say hello to the riders as they near so that the horse realises that you are not a threat.

Rivers

Some dogs love water and will think nothing of plunging in the river. With the extreme weather conditions over the last few years a river that may be safe for your dog to swim in can change in a matter of hours to become a swollen torrent that could wash your dog away. Please be careful when near rivers if there have been heavy periods of rain or if they look swollen or fast flowing.

The Lake District National Park

The Lake District Naional Park was formed in 1951 to protect the beauty of the mountainous landscape and tranquil lakes from being developed into housing and industry. Most of the National Park is owned privately. Roughly 25% belongs to the National Trust and only 3.9% belongs to the Lake District National Park Authority.

The villages and farmland only add to the beauty which complement the natural landscape, with its heathlands, hedgerows and beautifully crafted stonewalls that are blanketed in moss and the quaint cottages and beautiful houses that have been built from local stone.

Ground Nesting Birds

During 1st March through to end of July there will be several species of birds that make their nest on the ground. Dogs can disturb or harm chicks if they roam amongst the heather and bracken. During this time it is essensial to keep your dog on the paths whilst walking amongst the heathland and grassland areas.

Birds in the United Kingdom are split into three categories of conservation importance - Red, Amber and Green. Red being the highest conservation priority, with species needing urgent action. Amber is the next most critical on the list followed by green. For more information on this please see the BTO or RSPB websites.

Birds that will be breeding on the Red data list include Sky lark, Twite and Hen harriers. Birds on the Amber list include Curlew, Snipe and Meadow pipits.

Livestock

If you find that you need to cross a field with cattle and they seem interested in you or your dog it is recommended by the Countryside Code to let your dog off the lead. Never try to get between cattle and your dog. Your dog will get out of a situation a lot easier with speed than you can. It is usually only cattle with young calves that can be a threat. Or young heifers or bullocks that tend to get a little inquisitive. They will usually stop when they get close to you or your dog.

If you encounter horses and they seem to get aggressive towards your dog, the Countryside Code recommends you let the dog off the lead. Most horses will come over for a fuss but a small per cent do have a problem with dogs and will see them as a threat and will act to defend the herd. Horses that are out with a rider are completely different as they are not defending the herd and as long as you keep a safe distance there will not be a problem.

Sheep are not a danger to you but your dog can be a danger to them. Where sheep are grazing it is vital that you have your dog on a lead or under very close control. You will know your dog but if you are unsure better to play safe and keep your dog on a lead.

Forests

The forest walks in this book are a changing landscape, which makes them unique and interesting. Descriptions may change with time, for instance a path may be described as being in the shade of the forest, but as this is a worked forest a section could be clear felled at any time. Another change over the years could be where a view is described across a previously felled area. This could then be planted up and trees grown blocking the views. Paths may change but this is less likely. On rare occasions the Forestry Commission may temporarily close paths due to forest works but again this is even less likely on a weekend. Any changes to the path networks that may occur after the date of print will be updated on our website.

1. Great Langdale

Easy - 2.7 miles - 1hr

This is a great walk, walking part of the Cumbrian Way towards Chapel Stile and back along the centre of the valley with stunning scenery of the Langdale Pikes. Plenty of water along the way for your dog but sheep on half of the walk so you may need dogs on leads. A very small section of road.

How to get there - From Ambleside, follow signs for Coniston on the A593. Continue on the B5343 following signs for Great Langdale. About 3-4 miles from Chapel Stile.

Grid Ref - NY 294 064
Nearest Post Code - LA22 9JU

Parking - Either in the National Park car park or the National Trust car park. Pay and Display.

Facilities - There are toilets in the National Trust Car Park and a lovely dog friendly pub the Stickle Barn.

You will need - Dog leads, dog bags

The Walk

1 Dogs on leads to begin with. From the National Park car park with your back to the road take the path on the left in the far corner. From the National Trust car park go to the furthest end from the entrance and pass the toilet block having it on your left. Walk past the front of the Stickle Barn pub. Go through the pub car park onto the drive and turn right. Once reaching the road cross over and enter the National Park car park. Take the footpath on your left in the far corner.

Once on this path it is safe to let your dog off the lead. The path goes for some distance in the valley between stock fencing with some remnant hedge trees on either side.

As you near the end of the track get your dog back on the lead. Once at the end turn left onto another farm track. **2** Once at the road turn right for a short distance. Take the footpath through the kissing gate on the right.

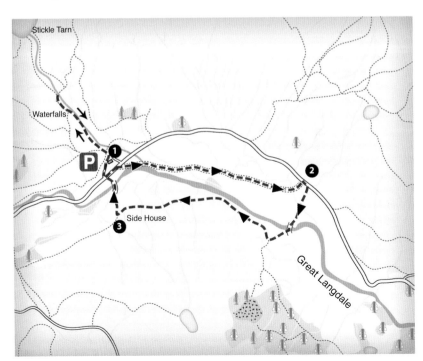

You can let your dogs off the lead here for a short while as you walk between the hedgerows. Note the traditional stone slab field boundaries. Pass through another kissing gate putting your dogs on leads or under close control and follow the obvious track.

Cross a stream/ditch and through another kissing gate. Go along the middle of the field on the track and through another kissing gate over a bridge and through another kissing gate.

Follow the farm track up the hill towards the farmhouse. Pass the farmhouse on your right. Turn right passing a stone barn. Stay between the stonewalls for a while. You are following the long distance footpath the Cumbrian Way.

The path goes downhill and through a kissing gate. Stay on this path, which goes uphill again becoming very stony. The views are fantastic of the Langdale Pikes. You will be walking between the hillside and a stonewall.

Passing many glacial boulders along the way following the stonewall on your right. Cross a stone slab bridge over a stream and then enter a stone sheep fold, which is a fine example of traditional craftsmanship.

Back out of the keep through a gate. It is all downhill from now on. Follow the stone path as you descend the field heading for the kissing gate. Once through the kissing gate continue straight ahead and pass a gap in the stonewall.

You must put your dogs on leads now as you approach the farm house. Walk alongside a stream on your right. Go over the small bridge and through a kissing gate keeping the buildings to your left.

❸ Pass through the farm gate and down the access path crossing through the middle of a field. Go over a bridge to the road and then to your car park. Straight on for the National Trust car park or right along the road for a little way to the National Park car park.

2. Elterwater

Medium - 3.6 miles - 1.5hr

Elterwater is a very appealing little village with chocolate box cottages and beautiful scenery. A partial river walk surrounded by woodland and glorious views of the hills as you approach the head of a valley. Crossing some farmland and a very quiet access track with some stunning ancient woodland on either side. There are plenty of opportunities for your dog to get a cooling drink along the way and a great dog friendly pub the Wainwrights, which is well recommended, making it an ideal place to stop for lunch. There are sheep and cattle for a small section of the walk.

How to get there - From Ambleside take the A593 to Clappersgate and then follow the signs for Elterwater on the B5343. Once in the village turn left just before the Britannia Inn and park in the National Trust Car Park.

Grid Reference - NY 328048

Nearest Post Code - LA22 9HP

Parking - Pay and display

Facilities - Toilets in the Car Park

You will need - Dog Leads, dog bags

The Walk

❶ Dogs will need leads to begin with. From the Car Park go back to the road and turn left going over the bridge. Have a look over both sides of the bridge at the stunning clear water and the green colours of the stone riverbed.

Once across the bridge turn right up the hill on the quiet road. Follow this road, which parallels the river to your right and below. Once you see an underground quarry entrance on your left take the right path into the woods. This is quite rocky, and goes down hill to the river. It is best to keep your dog on the lead here, as the river current is strong.

Follow the path alongside the river through the mature Oak woods. Once passing a gap in the stonewall where there was once a gate it is safe to let your dog off the lead. The river has been damned here and is much calmer. A little further along there is a nice stone bench, which is perfect to sit and enjoy the river.

Continue along the path and take the footbridge across the river. Dogs must go back on the leads now, as once through the wooden gate there is a road. Turn left on the road passing the Wainwright's. This pub is dog friendly so you are welcome to call in here.

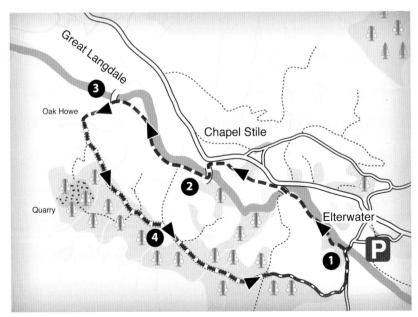

Once past the pub take the footpath on the left and walk between the stonewalls. You will pass a farm building on the left. At the junction go left and pass the farmhouse and through the gate, keeping the house on your left.

Walk along the side on the obvious path and through a small wooden gate and walking between two stonewalls. At the junction turn left and over a stone bridge. ❷

Take the gate on the left to avoid the cattle grid. Stay on this stone path, which follows the river and passes the edge of the Baysbrown Camp Site. There are stunning views here where it appears like you are entering the end of the valley with hills on three sides.

Pass through a series of kissing gates along this stone farm track. ❸ It will then veer left and head up towards the farmhouse. Pass the house and when reaching a stone barn turn left across a rocky field.

Walking alongside the stonewall on the right. As the stonewall bends to the right take the path left. Crossing little streams, which are flowing off the hillside to your right.

Go through a farm gate between a stonewall and cross stepping-stones over a stream. It is downhill now passing a stone animal keep on the left.

Through a gate passing a large rock on your right. Uphill and into the mixed woodland, passing lots of rocky outcrops. Keep on this path downhill passing a path right that goes uphill.

④ Pass through a farmyard walking between the farm buildings and follow the quiet sealed road ahead. Ignore the footpath on the left and continue uphill.

You will soon be walking between mature deciduous woodland that is predominantly Oaks, where everything is carpeted in green moss and ferns. There are lots of freshwater streams along this road for dogs to take a drink.

Ignore the bridleway on the right and pass a house on the left and ignore the bridleway to the left. Continue on downhill between the mossy stonewalls.

Pass another house on the left and then ignore the footpath on the right. You will pass a house on the right and then passing Elterwater Hall.

Once at the end of the road turn left and pass houses on the left then over the stone bridge and back to your car.

3. Loughrigg Tarn

Challenging - 5.5 miles - 3hrs

This is one of our walks where we would recommend you take a packed lunch and make a day of it, as it is not one to be rushed. There are so many places that you may want to stop, relax and take in the views or let your dog splash around in the water. You will have a couple of demanding climbs to begin with but the views here are not to be missed looking over Grasmere and Windermere. There is a lovely waterfall, woodlands, a river and two water bodies making a delightful day for you and your dog. There may be sheep grazing on this walk.

How to get there - From Ambleside take the A593 to Skelwith and then take the B5343 for Elterwater turning on the left, signed Little Langdale and Colwith. You will find parking just on the left after you have turned onto the road.

Grid Reference - NY 328 048

Nearest Post Code - LA22 9HN

Parking - Free in the car park

Facilities - Public toilets at the Village of Elterwater.

You will need - Dog leads, dog bags

The Walk

❶ Dogs on leads as the road is busy ahead and there may be sheep grazing. From the Car Park at the entrance to the road go right.

Once reaching the main road cross at the junction and follow the grass track on the opposite side of the road. Follow the incline and once at the stonewall turn with the path left.

Cross a stream where your dog can get water, then when meeting another path go right ignoring the path straight ahead. Continue on your ascent on the grassy track with the stonewall to your right.

The stonewall will soon veer right and you will reach a track to the left and a track straight on. Take the track straight on following up the hill. There is a quiet road up ahead.

At the road go right on the obvious track. Dogs can find water on the left of the track here. Just before you reach the stonewall take the track on the left, where you will cross the road. Continue uphill on the footpath ahead. Keep to the narrow path until you reach the rocky outcrops.

You will have beautiful views on a clear day if you turn around once reaching the rock. You can stop and rest a while soaking up the views. The path veers

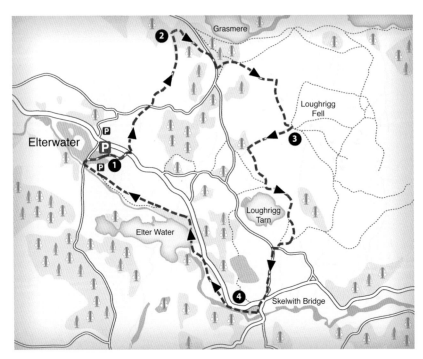

to the right here. There is a grassy area as you reach a plateau.

Continue on where you will see two obvious paths ahead. Take the one to the right and not up towards the rocks. Staying with the edge of the rock to your left. Walking towards two stonewalls, you will start to descend a little.

Pass through a gate where you will be met with stunning scenery, having tremendous views over Grasmere. Dogs will find water here. Follow down the valley between two stonewalls. The path will bend sharply to the left where you meet with the stonewall.

Pass through the gate and start to descend but go through the gate on your right almost immediately. Dogs can be let off the lead here. ❷ Walking across the wooded hillside where there are stunning views to your left.

Go through the metal gate ahead and as you pass the second ornate metal bench put your dog back on the lead, as you will be approaching a road ahead. Once reaching the road turn right.

Look out for the footpath/bridleway on your left signed Loughrigg Terraces. You will notice the unique design for fence posts at the stonewall on your left. Continue down this path ignoring the path on the right and back.

Ignore the path on the left and go through the kissing gate ahead, (there may be sheep grazing here) crossing the stream and then take the steps on the right ❸ for your final climb which will bring you the most outstanding views of Grasmere and once over the other side of the hill you will have views of Windermere. Remember to look back once in a while to get your breath back and take in the view.

Once near the top the landscape opens out where there are many hilltops. Keep walking ahead on the obvious track heading for the trig point, which is a stone cone on the highest point.

Once you are at the trig point pass it and go down the hill on the other side. You will see views of Windermere here on a clear day. Veer right just before the Cairn (rock pile), now following the path with views of Elter Water.

This can be a steep descent and will have steps in places. Take care if you have your dog on a lead so that you are not pulled over. It may be safer if there are no sheep about to let your dog off the lead if you can keep him under close control.

There are juniper bushes here, which are rare and one of only three coniferous trees native to Britain the others being Yew and Scots Pine. As you near the bottom of the hill you will meet a stonewall. Take the gate on the left here and follow the path. Passing a gap in the stonewall and continue ahead towards Loughrigg Tarn.

When reaching a gate on the right after estate fencing go through and down to the track turning left. You are safe to let your dogs off leads here but listen for traffic as there is access for a house.

Follow the estate fencing passing a gate on the right. As you reach another gate on your right you can either go through the gate and cross the field diagonally to the left heading for a kissing gate or stay on the track if you want to avoid any stock that may be in the field and continue walking around the field.

Passing the tarn on the right and if you have gone through the field go over the stile where your dog can go through the lift gate. Once back on the track go right and continue walking between the estate fencing.

You will pass a campsite and a house on the right then go through a gate putting your dog back on the lead. Ignore the path to the left, then when reaching a fork immediately ahead go right towards another house. Passing a row of cottages on your right then turn left at the road junction.

At another fork go right walking along the quiet road. When you reach the road junction turn left. Pass a parking bay on your left and a river. Continue walking down the road and pass another house on your left. There will be a very busy road ahead.

Once you reach the main road don't go first right but go right along the main road. Head towards Skelwith Bridge sign and follow on the pavement/track along the main road. Pass the Skelwith hotel and turn right towards the footpath signed Elterwater. Pass the cottages following the road between houses. Pass the old mill buildings. Stay on this path with the river to your left. It is best to keep your dog on the lead, as there is a gap in the wall ahead, which leads to a road.

❹ Keeping your dog on the lead go down the steps on the left if you wish to view the magnificent waterfall. Back on the path and continue ahead. You will pass a bridge on the left, which is a super design. Don't go over the bridge but straight ahead and through the kissing gate into the meadows.

Stay on the stone track along the river, keeping dogs on leads or under close control as there may be sheep grazing. It is idyllic here with views of the hills ahead framed by trees.

The river will widen and you will be then looking over Elter Water. Sit a while and enjoy the water with your dog, you have earned the rest. Continue on and go through a gate walking along the water in the canopy of trees.

The path joins the river again as you leave Elter Water behind. Cross a small wooden bridge and you will have plenty of pebble beaches where you can enjoy the river's edge.

You will have rolling hills to your right criss-crossed with stonewalls as they tumble up and down marking the field boundaries.

As you see the Car Park go through a gate putting your dog on the lead as this path goes to the road ahead. You are now in the village of Elterwater. Once at the road go right and follow the road round which bends right. Walking up this road you will reach the Car Park.

4. Easedale Tarn

Medium - 4.5 miles - 2.5hrs

This walk is truly amazing with stunning scenery and a waterfall named Sourmilk that grows as you get closer to it. There is a gradual hill for some of the walk but nothing too steep. The climb is much rewarded on a clear day as the views are breath taking and once at the top you will be met with Easedale tarn, which is very atmospheric amongst the hills, where your dog can enjoy the water. This walk is a linear so you will have the option of turning round at any point but this is not recommended as you will miss out on so much. There are sheep on this walk and some quiet roads. Lots of water for your dog.

How to get there - Take the A591 for Keswick and follow signs for Grasmere. Turn onto the B5287 and pass the first car park and follow signs for the car park in the village

Grid Reference - NY 336073

Post Code - LA22 9TA

Parking - Pay and display in Broadgate car park

Facilities - There are toilets in Grasmere

You will need - Dog leads, dog bags

The Walk

1 Dogs on leads to begin with. From the car park go back onto the road and turn right then immediately left. Pass the hotel on the right and a row of cottages. Take the first road on the left passing some houses and head towards the nice gate entrance taking the gate on the left of the road to avoid the cattle grid.

There may be sheep grazing here. Head back onto the driveway and take the footpath on the right. Follow this path towards the white house. Pass the house and continue straight ahead and through the kissing gate. You may let your dog off the lead here. Walk between the stock fence and the hedgerow, which is beech, to begin with.

At the end of this path, put your dog on the lead and go through the gate and turn left onto the quiet road. Stay on this road until you see a footbridge on the left, which crosses the river. **2** This is just before you reach Oak Lodge. Once across the footbridge go straight ahead through the trees and over another smaller stone footbridge.

Follow this path straight on with a stream on your right. Pass a footbridge on the right and continue straight ahead with a stonewall on your left. Ignore the footpath to the left. The stonewall will end to be replaced with a stock fence.

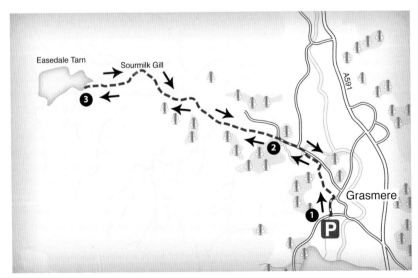

Go through a gate and take the left fork towards Sourmilk gill. Walk straight on through the middle of the field on the stoned path. Go through another gate and pass some rocky boulders.

Pass through a kissing gate and then straight on ascending with a stonewall on your right. Cross a stream as it washes over the rocks via a wooden footbridge. The scenery is stunning in all directions here.

Continue uphill where you will soon meet with Sourmilk gill, the stunning waterfall. On each side of the river you will see some Juniper amongst the holly, which is native but rare in Britain.

As you continue uphill the area flattens out and opens up. You are almost at the furthest point of the walk. A little more ascent and you will reach the tarn following on the worn grassy path.

❸ Once at the tarn it is time for a well earned rest as you absorb the wonderful atmosphere and scenery. Once you are ready it's back down the way you came. Remember to turn right once you reach the quiet road and look out for the gate on the right. This path runs parallel to the road for a time.

Once through the kissing gate at the end of this path ignore the footpath to the right towards the house and continue on the path meeting with the driveway, turning left and through the gate at the side to avoid the cattle grid. At the end of this road turn right and continue to the end where you will see the car park once more.

5. Grasmere

Medium - 3.5 miles - 1.5hrs

This is a beautiful walk and for those dogs that like water it will be a real treat, following rivers and Grasmere. There is stunning scenery with views that will take your breath away, and fantastic broadleaved woodlands. There is a small section where sheep may be grazing and a couple of quiet roads for short distances. Please watch that the river is not swollen, as after long periods of rain rivers can be dangerous for your dog.

How to get there - From the A591 from Ambleside pass through Rydal and park at the White Moss Car Park, which is located on the left hand side of the road.

Grid Ref - NY 349 065

Nearest Post Code - LA22 9SE

Parking - Pay and display in White Moss car park

Facilities - There are toilets signed from the car park

You will need - Dog leads, dog bags

The Walk

1 From the car park go to the furthest end and take the path that runs parallel with the road then onto a main path with the river on the left. You can let your dogs off the leads here. Go over a small bridge and then ignore the path to the right.

Once reaching the river take the kissing gate on the right just before the bridge. Stay on this path with the river on the left crossing the meadow. Go through a gate where the woods thicken.

Pass through another gate into Penny Rock wood, taking the path straight on up the hill through the woods that are predominantly Oak and Beech. Loughrigg Fell is on your left.

The path descends, veering left towards a bridge across the river. Go through a gate and then right towards Grasmere lake and weir. Follow along the edge of the water where your dog may enjoy a dip to cool off.

Pass through another gate and follow the main path through the woods keeping close to the water's edge. Ignore a path to the left and keep going straight ahead though the mixed broadleaves.

The path leaves the woodland with a field to the left. Follow the lake path where you will pass an old stone boathouse jutting into the water. This is a lovely quiet lake where you can enjoy stunning views across the water.

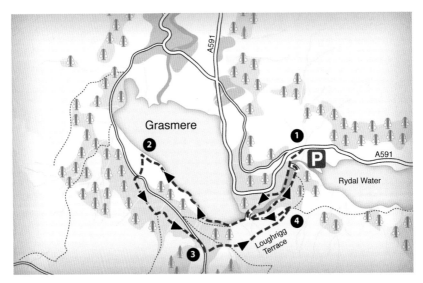

Cross over a footbridge and then go left, ❷ walking between fields. As you see a stonewall put your dog on the lead. Continue up the hill through a gate onto the quiet road turning right.

Take the sealed path on the left at a cottage where it is safe to let your dog off the lead, but this is an access track so listen for traffic. Pass Huntingstile Lodge on the left.

Leave the sealed track and join the cobble path up the hill between green cloaked walls. Ignore a stile on the right and continue up the hill. At the top of the hill take the iron gate on the left, signed Loughrigg Terrace.

Follow the path through broadleaved woodland with great views of Grasmere to the left. Go through a gate onto a bracken hillside. After the second bench on the right put your dog on the lead as you near a quiet road. At the road go right and a little further on take the footpath on the left. ❸

Descend between stonewalls with a unique stile of fence post anchors on the left. Ignore the footpath on the left and go through a gate. There may be sheep grazing here. Continue straight ahead over a stream following Loughrigg Terrace. The views are amazing on the left here over Grasmere and beyond. Sit on the benches and rest a while taking it all in.

Continue on this path as it descends, passing over another stream. Ignore the path that veers right up the hill and continue straight ahead on your descent. As you reach a stonewall turn left and continue down the hill. ❹

Keep to the stonewall on the right heading back towards the lake. At the fork head towards the bridge on the right. When you reach the path at the bridge don't go over the bridge but go right walking with the river edge to your left.

Go through the kissing gate into White Moss wood. Stay on the path through the trees, which are Alder Carr woodlands, keeping to the river on the left. The path starts to incline when reaching the denser woodland and moves away from the river.

As the path descends again it meets back with the river and soon you will see a bridge on the left. Cross this bridge to the other side of the river. Put your dog back on the lead once more and continue straight ahead to the car park.

6. Rydal

Medium- 3.5 miles -1.5hr

This walk is packed with things to interest us all. Walking through woodlands alongside streams and rivers. Passing the historic home of William Wordsworth, and Rydal Hall and gardens where you can visit the dog friendly tearoom for lunch and explore the traditional gardens with a wonderful waterfall. Resting again in the peace and tranquility whilst absorbed with views over Rydal water then passing an awe-inspiring cave. Plenty of water for dogs along the way. There are sheep grazing for parts of this walk and some roads.

How to get there - From the A591 from Ambleside pass through Rydal and park at the second White Moss Car Park, which is located on the right hand side of the road.

Grid Reference - NY 349 065

Post Code - LA22 9SE

Parking - Pay and Display

Facilities - There are toilets on the opposite side of the main road crossing at the entrance to the Car Park and turning left. Part way around there is a dog friendly teashop at Rydal Mount.

You will need - Dog leads, dog bags

The Walk

❶ Dogs on leads to begin with. From the Car Park facing the rock, take the footpath at the right hand side of the Car Park and follow adjacent to the road. Turn left and back track a little going back towards the Car Park but ascending into the woods.

Once you are away from the road it is safe to let your dog off the lead. There is a slightly steep ascent here and is probably the most challenging hill in the walk. As the hill becomes a little steeper you may wish to get your dog on a lead. You will reach a very quiet road at the top where you turn right. This track is known as the Coffin Route to Rydal.

Once passing a couple of cottages the road becomes a stone track. There is one more house ahead having access to this track but it is usually very quiet. It is safe to let your dog off the lead now.

You will walk between stonewalls and your dog will find water in several areas along the way. Ignore the footpath on your left. You will pass another house (Brockstone) on your left where the path veers right.

Ignore a path right and continue ahead and pass through a gate. Sheep may be grazing so keep your dog under close control. You will climb some steps/ rocks and go over a rocky outcrop.

Downhill now following the stonewall which bends sharply to the left and the path inclines here.

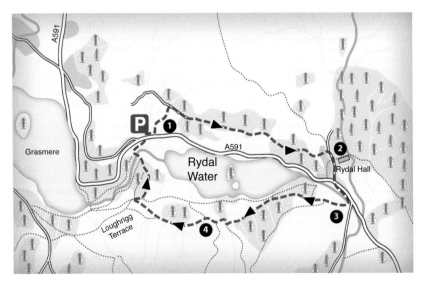

Go through a further kissing gate on your right, keeping to the path with the stonewall on your right. You will pass through a gate and over a stream. Look to the right for great views over Rydal Water.

You will pass a series of stone benches on your left looking out at the view. Pass through a gap in the stonewall. Go through a gate and to your left you will see an old stone water feeder. Keep on this path that descends passing under some mature ash and oak trees.

Pass a number of wind blown dead trees and a rocky outcrop to the left. Uphill again for a short spell and just before you reach the top there is another old stone water feeder on the right of the path, this time still working.

Pass through a field gate and continue forward. There is a quiet road ahead so before going through the next gate it is best to have dogs on leads. Go through the field gate with the gable end of the house that William Wordsworth once lived in on your right.

❷ As you reach the road go right downhill where on your left you will pass Rydal Hall and Gardens. This is well worth a visit at the dog friendly Tea Room where, although to a high standard, dogs can go inside. The gardens are also accessible to wander around and see the fine architecture of the hall. There is a waterfall and a quaint summerhouse.

Back on the road continue downhill to the main road. Here go left, crossing over the road and walking along the pavement until you reach a road on your right. Take this road and go over the bridge then directly right. ❸

Take the gate beside the cattle grid. Follow this access track passing Cote How Tea Room on your right and houses on your left. Go through a gateway where the path descends and bends sharply to the left. Dogs can be let off the lead here.

Go through a gate where you will have two choices. A. - Top path passing by a couple of caves or B. - Lower path passing Rydal Water where your dog can cool off.

Choice A. Veer left and take the top path walking above the water looking across the valley. The path will move left away from the lake where it becomes stony. Continue uphill into mixed woodlands.

Keep to the main path which goes over a stream, following a stonewall on your right. You will reach a rocky outcrop with a cave to your left. Keep walking along the path, which bends left as it inclines. The path will pass another cave on your left. This is stunning and in summer the echos of swallows as they chatter inside is a delight. ❹

Continue on the path descending amongst the bracken. There are views of the hills on all sides. When reaching a fork take the right path, which descends, and then another fork and again take the right path. The path then meets the lower lake path at an unusual stone and wooden kissing gate.

Choice B. Continue along the path to the right, which descends to the lake. Walk along the lakeside until it veers left. Keep on this path following the stonewall on your right. You will pass a ruined stone building on your right. Keep on the ascent where you will reach an unusual stone and wooden kissing gate where choice A. re-joins.

Go through the kissing gate and descend through the broadleaved woodland, steeped in moss. Head for the stonewall and walk alongside it under the canopy of trees.

Keep to the main path, which leads to a wooden bridge then cross the river. Dogs can cool off here. Once the dogs have enjoyed the river it is time for the leads as there is a busy main road ahead. Take the path left to the busy main road, crossing to the other side and into the Car Park.

7. Sweden

Medium - 3.5 miles - 1hr 45min

This is a lovely linear walk taking in the beautiful grounds of Rydal hall and its waterfall and woodlands, followed by a gradual climb with outstanding views of the glorious landscape and Windermere. There is water along the way, via the river, once leaving the access track to the hall. There are sheep grazing on this walk.

How to get there - From Ambleside take the A591 towards Grasmere and follow the sign for Rydal Hall on the left.

Grid Reference - NY 364063

Post Code - LA22 9LX

Parking - On the roadside

Facilities - There is a fantastic dog friendly tea shop in the grounds of the hall.

Things you will need - Dog leads, dog bags

The Walk

❶ Dogs on leads to begin this walk. Go into the entrance of Rydal hall following the footpath sign between two stonewalls signed to the tea shop, which is the last entrance near to the top of the hill. Head towards several buildings, passing the teashop on your left, which is dog friendly. Cross over a bridge and continue on between buildings.

Turn right walking past a parking bay on your right. Go straight on and then left walking through the ornamental gardens of Rydal hall. Go through the farm gate and along the quiet access track between the stock fencing where you can let your dogs off the leads. Listen for traffic on this path.

As you pass between the fields you will see the lovely mature parkland trees on either side. Just before you meet with a river on your left go through an iron gate. **❷** You will hear the river before you see it. Proceed up the hill through woods with the river to your right.

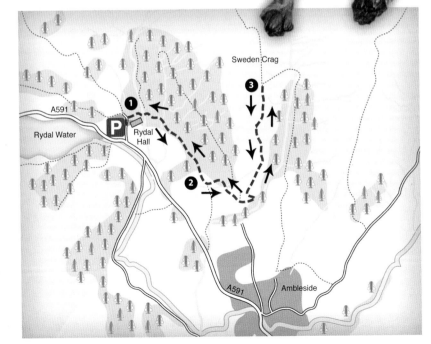

Pass through another gate where you will need to put your dogs on leads as you enter a field where stock may be grazing. Follow on the path with the stonewall to your right.

You will reach a path ahead where you turn left. Look to your right for fantastic views of Windermere. Continue up the hill following a stoned track. Pass through a gate and turn left following the stonewall on your left.

Pass through a gap in the stonewall where you will pass under a mature oak tree continuing on the obvious stone path. You will have views of the Langdales to your left.

Pass through another gap in the stonewall and the path will then bend to the right. Keep to the more obvious stoned track. The path will veer left and right, take the right path. Head for a further gap in the stonewall. Once through the gap you will see an animal keep to your right. ❸

This is the furthest point of your walk. Turn around for fantastic views of Windermere. You will enjoy these views as you descend back in the direction that you came. Remember to turn right after the sharp bend once at the stonewall with the river behind it. Back through the gate by the river where you can let your dog off the lead.

Once back on the access path to Rydal Hall go right and continue straight on passing through the gate as before. Dogs back on leads. Do not go right passing the parking bay but continue on passing through a gate to go over a bridge where you will have views of the wonderful Lower Rydal Beck waterfall.

Pass the stunning Rydal hall to your right and continue straight ahead taking a left path near a car park and out through the gate back on the road where you have parked your car.

8. Skelghyll Woods

Medium - 5 miles - 2.5hrs

This is a lovely walk through woodlands onto a limestone outcrop with fabulous views over Windermere and beyond, passing farmyards and along farm tracks and quiet lanes. It is a great opportunity to see the beauty of this surrounding area with all its peace and tranquility. There are a few gradual hills with a couple of steeper sections. Your dog will find lots of water along the way. There are sheep grazing for half of this walk.

How to get there - From Ambleside heading on the A591 towards Windermere go into the car park just on the edge of Ambleside on the left next to the Fisherbecks Hotel.

Grid Reference - NY377038

Nearest Post Code - LA22 0DH

Parking - Pay and Display Car Park

Facilities - There are no facilities

You will need - Dog leads, dog bags

The Walk

① From the car park go to the furthest end away from the main road which will lead you on to a quiet road. Go right here and look for a road on your left, just before a house. Continue uphill where you will be met with stunning views of Windermere.

Take the road on the right, which is signed Skelghyll woods. This is a surfaced access road to houses but is very quiet so you may wish to let your dog off its lead here. Keep a watch for cars.

You will pass a bench and then further on your dogs will find water on your right. Keep to the main path following a stonewall. Once entering the woods at the end of the stonewall turn left. Follow this path, which ascends through the mixed broadleaved woodland with some conifers. The path becomes rocky underfoot.

Cross a bridge over the river and continue uphill. **②** Once at a plateau you will see a path to your right a little further on which is a short detour over Jenkins Crag, a limestone outcrop for absolutely stunning views across Windermere and the Langdale Pikes. Then back on the path turning right to continue your walk.

There are many areas for your dog to find water along this section as it crosses under the path. The woods here are all deciduous dominated by Oaks. The path ascends once more and a little further on will meet with a stonewall on the right which is blanketed in moss.

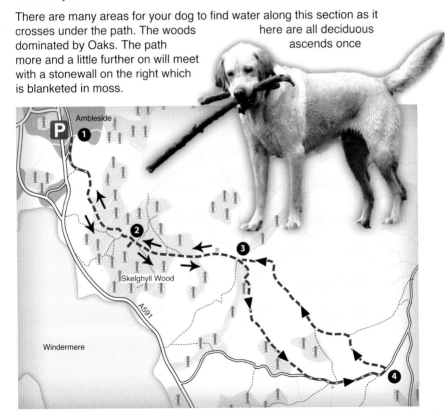

As you leave the stonewall behind the woods clear on your right to enable you to see the wonderful Windermere once more as you look across the fields. Pass through the gate where you will need to get your dogs on leads, as there is stock grazing.

Stay on the obvious track where you will pass through a further gate. Pass a house on the left and then through another gate across the farmyard. Continue along the access track and once reaching a fork on the track go left taking the path signed for Troutbeck. Go through the gate to avoid the cattle grid and continue straight ahead through the field gate not left, passing through fields on a sealed road. ❸

Go through another gate, passing a farm building on the right and a house on the left. Through a further gate passing through fields where you descend on a sealed track. Just after the farm building on the right pass through a gate onto a quiet access road where you may wish to let your dog off the lead but keeping a watch for traffic.

Your dog will find water on the left on the other side of the gate. Pass a house on your left called Close Cottage then be sure to get your dog on the lead before reaching a road ahead once you pass a farm building on the left.

Once reaching the road turn left. This is a fairly quiet road but it is best to keep your dog on the lead. Ignore the footpaths on your left and right at the farm and continue along the road for a while turning left on the bridleway just before the lay-by on the right hand side of the road. ❹ You can let your dogs off the leads again. This path is quite stony and will ascend passing a stone barn and then go through a series of gates. When reaching the junction put dogs back on leads and turn left on the quiet road and continue uphill. Your dog will find water on the right here before it goes under the path.

Follow on this road for a short way and then go through a kissing gate to the left and not the farm gate straight ahead. Proceed downhill then through a gateway following the stonewall on your left. You will have views ahead and left of the hills. Passing a copse of trees on your left continue straight ahead. Go through a gate and walking straight on keeping with the stonewall. You will cross a stream where your dog can get water. You will cross another stream walking straight on between the stonewalls.

Follow the path down the middle of the field and then through a gate at the stream and then passing through another gate then go right and through a kissing gate to avoid the cattle grid.

Continue straight ahead ascending on this familiar path towards the farmhouse. Passing once again through the farmyard. Continue as before towards the woods. Once reaching the woods remember to keep to the main stony path, ignoring the path that veers to the right.

Cross the footbridge once again and continue your descent through the trees. Once at the end of the access path and back onto the road turn left to proceed downhill. Once meeting with another road go right and back to the car park.

9. Coniston

Medium - 3 miles - 1hr

This is a truly delightful walk that you and your dog will enjoy. There are some roads to begin with as you walk through the village of Coniston. For the first half of the walk there may be sheep grazing and so if you have a cheeky dog it may be necessary to keep the lead on. The stunning scenery with rolling hills, moss covered walls, ancient trees and a folly will be really worth the effort. The second half of the walk however will be lead free passing through woodland with lots of clear water flowing through for your dogs.

How to get there - Head into Coniston on the A593. Once in the village, take the road on the corner of the Black Bull Hotel, heading for the Ruskin Museum. Pass the museum and a number of houses/buildings, parking a little further up the road beyond the yellow line.

Grid reference - SD 302979
Post Code - LA21 8DU

Parking - Free at the side of the road

Facilities - There are toilets in the car park in the village, which is signposted along the road.

You will need - Dog leads, dog bags

The Walk

❶ Dogs on leads to begin with. From your car head back down the road towards the village, passing the Ruskin museum. At the road junction, with The Black Bull on your right cross to the opposite side of the road and turn right.

Follow along the pavement, turning left crossing another road to the Crown Inn. Stay on this road passing houses on your left. Keep on this road until you see Shepards Bridge Lane on your left. Turn onto this road passing a social club on your right.

❷ Take the footpath on the right and over a bridge then left before the house. Through the kissing gate and follow the path along the fence line and the river heading for the gate.

Do not go through the gate but alongside the wall to the right. Pass under a large oak tree and head for the folly ahead. Go through the kissing gate to the left of the folly.

Take the path to the right of the field and follow the fence line uphill and through the gate. Keep to the obvious grassy path. Look back for lovely views over Coniston. Ignore the path to the right and continue forward towards a traditional stonewall.

Go through another kissing gate into the forest. Pass through the forest staying on the path and out through another gate.

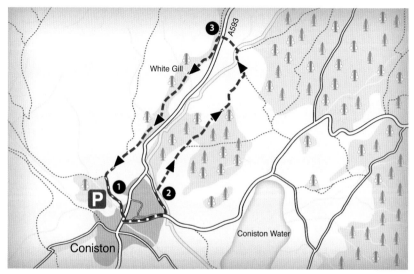

44

Continue along the obvious path, heading in a straight line to a gate on the opposite end of the field. Passing through some lovely old parkland trees, scrub, Silver Birch and rocky outcrops. You will see stunning scenes to your left of the hills. Pass through the gate and continue straight ahead. Walking near to a stonewall and passing some mature Oaks you will see another gate ahead and left.

Once through the kissing gate turn left where you can now let your dog off the lead. You will see a river on your left and a little further on there is an opening so that your dog can gain access for a drink. Take care that the water flow is not strong, if so put your dog on the lead before allowing him access to the river.

Just before you pass over a stone bridge put your dog on the lead and pass a stone barn on your right, there is a busy main road ahead. Keep walking on down the drive towards the road.

❸ Cross the road to enter the footpath on the opposite side and through the kissing gate. Turn left on this woodland path where it is safe to let your dog off the lead. Take care if you have an energetic dog as the wall is low and keeps to the road for a little while.

You will pass through a gap in the stonewall. Ignore the kissing gate left and continue forward. The path will now leave the road so you can relax. There is an interesting rock face to your right. All along this path you will see rocks and trees blanketed in moss, ferns galore and clear water inlets for your dog.

You will cross several footbridges across streams and ignore a further kissing gate on the left. A little further on you will see a gate. Before going through this gate put your dog back on the lead as sheep may be grazing.

You will see the rocky hills to your right and a stonewall on your left. Ignore the gate on your left and continue a little further until you reach a gate ahead. Go through the gate onto the road and turn left. Continue down this road passing some houses and soon reaching your car.

10. Tom Gill

Medium - 5.5 miles - 2hrs 30min

This is a splendid walk that begins by following a river upstream with waterfalls, the largest being Tom Gill, through woodland, meeting up with Tarn Hows. Through a forest onto farmland with stunning views all around of the beautiful countryside and hills, passing through woods and around the tranquil Yew Tree tarn. This walk has sheep grazing in parts.

How to get there - Take the A593 from Ambleside to Coniston and Tom Gill car park will be on the left hand side a good distance before reaching Coniston.

Grid Reference - SD 322998

Parking - National Trust Pay and Display

Facilities - There are no facilities on this walk

You will need - Dog leads, dog bags

The Walk

❶ From the car park take the path across the bridge, which is located on the right if you are facing the road. Go right through the gate and follow the stream uphill through mixed broadleaved woodlands, which are beautifully carpeted in mosses and ferns.

You will pass a small waterfall and the path will move away from the stream for a while. Stay on the obvious stony path. As you near the stream again you will come to the stunning Tom Gill waterfall. There are smaller waterfalls as you pass up steps/rocks where the water races downhill. Pass through a kissing gate and continue up hill. As you reach a wall ahead you will be coming to Tarn Hows.

❷ Once on the path at the tarn go left. Continue walking along the tarn for sometime where the path will ascend and descend as it moves away from the tarn. When you see an obvious stone path on your left signed Arnside and Langdales take this path leaving the tarn behind.

❸ The forest will open up with some grassland. Go through the kissing gate and turn right. Ascend on this path between stonewalls. There are views to

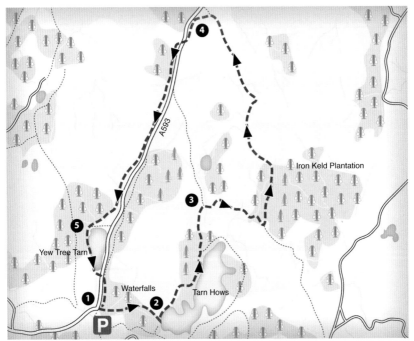

your right of Tarn Hows, with views of the Langdales on the left. You will see a kissing gate on your left, just before going through have a look behind you at the views. Stay to the main path passing rocky outcrops on your right and views to your left. The path goes uphill, continue straight ahead ignoring the path on the right. Put your dogs on leads or keep them under close control and pass through a kissing gate out of the woods into farmland, where you will be met with stunning views of the Langdale pikes.

Downhill now passing through a gate and continue straight on. The path goes close to a farm house on the left. Then shortly after, go through a gap in the stonewall. The views are truly stunning here of the Langdale valley. Take the left path at the way marker, keeping near to the stonewall on the left. Go through the gate on the left and then take the right turn. Follow the stonewall on the right. A little further on ignore the gate on the right and continue straight on. The path now ascends a little. Put your dogs on leads before passing through the gate as there is a busy road ahead.

❹ The path runs parallel with a road, then will meet with the road. Cross over and enter into a quiet road on the opposite side. Take the first footpath on the left almost immediately. Go through a kissing gate on your right and follow the footpath that runs parallel with the road. Pass through a kissing gate and over a footbridge. You will reach a road further along. Cross the road and back through another kissing gate and continue to follow the path running parallel with the road walking amongst the trees.

Go through a further kissing gate and then over a footbridge. You will meet with another road, cross the road and go through the kissing gate on the opposite side. Again this path runs parallel with the road, passing rocky hills to your right.

Pass through another kissing gate and continue straight on, ignoring a kissing gate on your left a little further on just after reaching the trees. Cross a stream using the stones that are placed. You will cross a footbridge and then pass a sheep fold on your left. Continue straight ahead passing a wooded hillside to your right and rocky crags. Pass through a gap in the stonewall, walking with a stream to your left and the stonewall to your right, it is now safe to let your dog off the lead. ❺ Passing through mixed woodlands ignoring a footbridge on your left and following the outer tarn path.

Pass through widely spaced trees then go through a kissing gate into woodland. As you follow the path you will see a path on the left going to the waters edge a little further on. You can stop a while here on the bench and have a rest. Your dog can cool off in the water. Continue on the path around the tarn putting your dog on the lead in good time as you are headed to the busy main road. Cross a bridge and turn right walking parallel with the road once again.

Cross the road and turn right heading for the obvious path ascending the hill through the trees to walk above the road keeping your dog on the lead, as there are no boundary fences at the road below. You will reach a familiar bridge which you cross then follow the path back to the car park.

Walk 10 - Tom Gill

11. Tarn Hows

Easy - 2.5 miles - 1hr

This is a lovely circular walk and very popular for dogs and families. Walking amongst trees and following along the waters edge around the tarn. Your dog will love dipping in and out of the water as you make your way around. With mixed woodland to one side of the tarn and a grazed area between two gates where there may be cattle. At the far end you will be in awe at the stunning scenery across the water and beyond.

How to get there - Take the B5286 to Hawkshead turning for Hawkshead Hill then following the signs for Tarn Hows. Ensure to park on the top car park nearest the lake.

Grid Reference - SD 326996

Parking - National Trust Car Park, Pay and Display (members free)

Facilities - There is a visitor centre and toilets

You will need - Dog Leads, dog bags

The Walk

1 From the car park take the path to the left and ahead. Once reaching the road take the path into Tarn Hows opposite the car park. Continue downhill and veer left and then right heading towards the lake.

At the lake go through the gate and continue straight ahead on the path, which will follow gentle little hills through the woods following the tarn to your right.

The trees here are mixed woodland. Ignore a path on your left when you come to it and continue straight ahead. Go through a gate and ignore the stile on your left. The path leads to a nicely crafted bench on your right looking over the water. Why not rest a while here. **2** You are just a little over half way round. There may be cattle grazing here for conservation purposes.

Cross a footbridge and continue your journey ahead. **3** Ignore a gate on the left some way along. You will soon have stunning views across the tarn and beyond.

After you pass though a gate take the path on the right and then the path on the left across the hillside. Once at the rock on the top of the hill look left and find your path back to the Car Park.

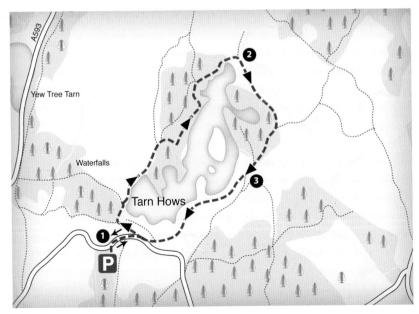

12. Hawkshead

Medium - 3.7 miles - 1hr 40min

This walk has beautiful panoramic views, woodlands, forests and grassland areas which are mainly stock free. There is plenty of opportunity for your dogs to quench their thirst and have a chance to run around without being restrained on leads. There are some roads at the beginning and the end but they are mostly quiet lanes. Sheep on the last section of the walk.

How to get there - Follow signs to Hawkshead and once arriving follow signs for the car park.

Grid Reference - SD 352 980

Parking - Pay and display

Facilities - There are toilets in the car park

You will need - Dog leads, dog bags

The Walk

1 Dogs on leads to begin this walk. At the entrance of the car park go right and once reaching the junction turn right. At another junction go left crossing the bridge. Just after the bridge take the road on the left signed Wray Castle, which is a much quieter road.

Pass between houses on the road then the road goes uphill with a sharp left bend. As the road levels out you will pass Crag Cottage on your right. Before you reach Gillbank on the right take the footpath on the right through the tall gate signed Belle Grange. **2**

Ascend on this stony track with mixed woodland following the fence line on the right. A stream will pass over the path where your dog can get a drink. You will leave the fence line as the track bends to the left.

Stay on this wider main path, which becomes a little rocky underfoot. The trees become widely spaced opening out to a bracken, grassland and gorse area. The path meets with a stonewall just before going through a gate. Your dog will find water here.

The trees are much more spaced out. Follow the path between the grass and bracken taking the left fork, which is the wider path. The path veers left where a stonewall appears on your right. Walking across the open grassland with gorse scrub and some trees, still on an ascent.

The path levels out and it becomes enclosed with larch trees. There is water here for your dog before going through a gate. Once through the gate continue on the path which will meet with a stonewall on the left a little further on and a stock fence on the right.

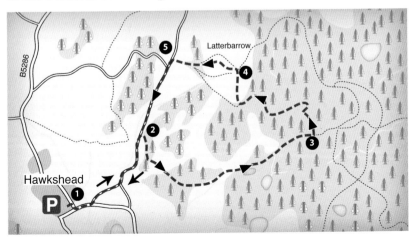

Pass through another gate where you will meet with a stonewall on your left. As you climb a little higher the views are outstanding ahead and to the left. When you reach the end of the stonewall and fence line take a left turn. ❸

Follow on this path which descends having a stonewall to your right at first but this will veer off to the right. Continue straight on heading for the stonewall in the distance.

Take the steps to the left when you see them on the steeper section as you near the stonewall. Once reaching the top go right. The path will follow a stonewall on your right for a short time and then bending sharply left will head for a fence line on the left a little further on. The surrounding area here has been clear felled of trees but has some young planted trees to take their place.

Keep on this obvious worn path, which will bend sharply right after a while. Ignore a footpath on the right a little further on and head for the gap in the stonewall which will take you into the forest.

Continue straight ahead where your dog will find water as it passes under the path. You will come to a stile on your right, which you will need to cross letting your dog through the lift gate provided.

There may be sheep grazing here so you may need to get your dog on the lead. Take the obvious path through the bracken to your right heading for your final up hill climb.

You will soon see a monument at the top of the hill. Once near the monument your next path will be found to the left side of the monument as you approach heading towards and through the middle of a rocky outcrop.

Before continuing take a look at the views from all sides they are really worth the climb. For the descent take care as it can get quite steep. It may be better to let your dog off the lead if there are no sheep in the area. ❹

Once near the bottom you will pass through a copse of trees where you will see a path. Go right at this path and continue on your descent. You will reach a gate where you need to put your dog on the lead, as you will be going on a quiet road. ❺

Go left and continue on this road where you will soon be on a familiar route. The road bends sharply to the right and you will again pass between houses. At the road turn right and cross the bridge, again turning right following the car park sign back to your car.

13. Wray Castle

Easy - 3 miles - 1hr

This is a great walk that you can amble along, sitting at the lake side enjoying the views at the water's edge, or for those of you that are pushed for time it can be done in an hour. It has fantastic views of the lake where your dog can cool off, great broadleaved trees giving some shade, and a castle. Plenty of water for your dog. There are sheep for a small section of the walk, with no roads except the castle access road.

How to get there - From the B5286 Ambleside to Hawkshead road follow the signs for Wray. Take the turning signed for Windermere and once you reach the lakeside Red Nab car park will be on your left.

Grid Ref - SD 386994

Parking - Free in Red Nab car park

Facilities - None

You will need - Dog leads, dog bags

The Walk

❶ From the car park go to the left hand side when you are facing the lake and take this lakeside path. Walking under the dappled shade of the trees where your dog will be free to dip in and out of the lake.

Pass a stone building that juts out into the water. There are some glorious mature Oaks with Hazel understory. You will then pass fields to your left with the characteristic stonewalls that flow with the hillsides.

A little further on there are woodlands to both sides again. Go through a gate ignoring the kissing gate on the left. Then as you pass through another gate you will see a gate on your right. **❷**

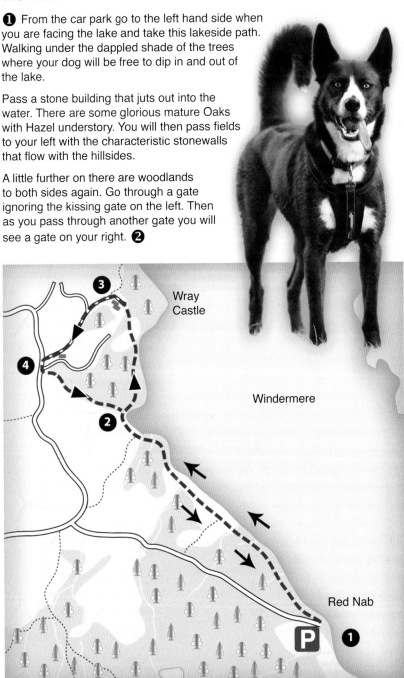

Take this gate checking for grazing animals, as you may need to put your dog on a lead and continue to follow the lake walking along the stone path to the edge of the hillside. This path will soon veer to the left away from the lake and ascending the hill.

Stay on the path as it snakes around, taking the route left to the castle towards the black estate fencing and gate, passing under the mature Oak tree. Put you dog on the lead here. Go through the gate and follow the path, which brings you through another gate towards the car park for the castle.

Keep to the right hand side along the edge of the trees and once out of the parking bays take the path on the right. Once reaching the estate fencing take the path to the left signed Blelham tarn.

Up the steps and right along the castle entrance path, taking care to look out for cars. Walking between the estate fencing with wonderful scenery. To your right you can see the two rugged peaks known as the Langdale Pikes. ❸

At the end of the path go left onto the road passing the castle gatehouse. ❹ Take the bridleway on the left and proceed between the stock fencing towards the lake.

You will soon recognise where you are, as this path will take you back to the car park if you retrace your steps going through the gates and keeping to the lake path.

14. Red Nab

Medium - 4.7 miles - 2hr

This walk has quite a steep hill, which is fairly long passing through some wonderful ancient woodland cloaked in mosses with abundant streams to help quench the thirst of your dog. Rocky outcrops covered in green with some windows through the woodland and forest, looking out on Windermere and beyond. Taking in some farmland and finishing with a fairly flat wooded path that passes near to the edge of Lake Windermere. It can be muddy in places, and rocky, hence strong footwear is essential. There may be sheep and cattle for a small section of this walk.

How to get there - Take the B5286 from Ambleside to Hawkshead. Take the left turn signed for Wray and continue to Red Nab car park signposted Windermere.

Grid Ref - SD 386994
Nearest Post Code - LA22 OJA

Parking - Free in Red Nab car park

Facilities - None

You will need - Dog leads, dog bags

The Walk

❶ From the Car Park face the lake and go right. Dogs can cool off here before they start. This is a quiet access track where you can let your dog off the lead but there may be cyclists.

❷ Once you have passed the large house on your right take the footpath on the right, signed Hawkshead into the woodland. This is a slab path that can be quite slippy and ascends for some way.

The woodland is steeped in mosses and ferns and has a real ancient feel to it with mature beech. As the path levels out take the footpath on the left signed for Far Sawrey. **❸** Cross over the stream and continue up hill, now on a rocky path.

The woodland changes here and becomes a forest of pines. At the fork take the higher path on the right. There are oaks and yews here mixed with pine. Pass over a stream where it gets quite muddy.

You will be walking the rocky path with forest to your right and woodland to your left. The path will level out as you reach the plateau. As the trees thin out you will see views to Windermere on your left.

Passing rocky outcrops cloaked in moss and streams a plenty with lots of Hazel understory and Oak, Silver Birch and Rowan trees this really is a delightful woodland. Passing bracken areas where the trees thin out.

Pass through a gap in the stonewall to enter a forest going downhill on the obvious path. Ignore a gap in the stonewall and follow straight on the path keeping close to the stonewall. At the finger post follow straight ahead signed Far Sawrey.

Pass several entrances in the stonewall. The path veers left and descends steeply where it can be tricky as you negotiate the rocky outcrop. Walking between the ancient stonewalls with high deer fencing.

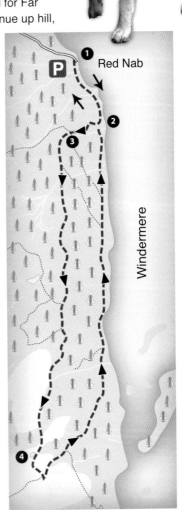

Go through a kissing gate into a clearing with rocky outcrops. There may be cattle here. Keep walking descending between the stonewall and grass bank. Pass through a gateway into a field, keeping to the left along side the stonewall.

Pass a pond on the right, which is good for dragonflies in the summer months. Head uphill and the path bends to the left walking between two stonewalls. As you approach the wooden farm gate ahead at the end of the stonewalls go left, ❹ following the bridleway signed Windermere Lake Shore.

Pass through a farm gate along the track between a field and a forest. Ignore the path on the right and continue straight on. Through another farm gate and along the path under the canopy of trees. The path becomes rocky descending into mixed woodlands. Ignore the path on the right walking with the forest to your right and deciduous woods on the left. Ignore the stile on the right where you see the boat mooring parking bay ahead. Pass over a stream, once reaching a track go left where you may let your dog back off the lead, as this road is very quiet, although there are cyclists.

Walk along this path for some time having some views and access to the lake in parts. The path eventually goes back to the Car Park.

15. Grizedale

Medium - 2.4 miles - 1hr 15min

This walk is a must for your dog as they can be off the lead for most of the time. There is just a small section of quiet lane and no livestock. There is also water in many places for your dog. There is a steady climb for a good part of the walk but the panoramic views on a clear day make it worth the hard work. In hot weather it is ideal under the shade of the forest trees.

How to get there – Grizedale Forest is signposted from Hawkshead village on the B5285.

Grid Ref - SD 335 945
Nearest Post Code - LA22 0QJ

Parking - Pay and Display

Facilities - Toilets, Visitor Centre, Cafe

You will need - Dog leads, dog bags

The Walk

❶ Dogs on the leads to begin with. From the car park go out of the main entrance and turn right on the forest road. Go over the bridge and then directly left. You can now let your dogs off the lead.

Keeping with the river on your left walk alongside a post and rail fence. Once at the end of the fence put your dogs on leads. Pass a wooden axe man on your right and veer towards the stone building.

Once reaching the stone building go left and go over the bridge. Facilities are on the left. Take the first right walking alongside the play area on your left. After the play area go diagonally left towards the entrance in the stonewall.

At the quiet road turn right and as you pass the house on your right ignore the path left through the gate but take the next left into the forest. **❷** Ascend the steps and your walk will be mostly uphill now for the first half. It is safe to let your dogs off lead here.

Following the red marker posts all the way. Walking through the deciduous woods at first and then walking through the forest. Once you reach the top of the path turn right onto the forest track. **❸**

Ignore the paths to the left and right and then take the next left. This is a stony path becoming a little rocky. The trees are deciduous again here. The path will get a little steeper as you incline.

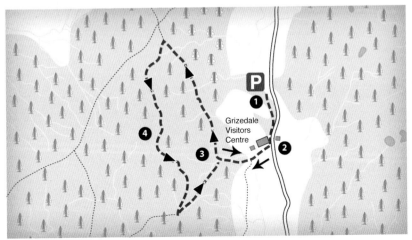

There is a little downhill as the path bends to the left. You will cross a stream by way of a tree stump and then look out for the path on the left.

Go left onto the forest track into a more open area where the forest has been clear felled. As you walk along this track turn round for views behind you. It will give you chance to get your breath back.

You will then have views to the left across the trees to the hills. Ignore the path to the right and continue ahead. When the track bends sharply left take the path on the right.

This is a steep ascent but you are nearly at the top. It opens out at the top with some rocks and heathland where you will see the trig point marking the highest viewpoint. It is a bit of a scramble here, but a must to see the fantastic panoramic views. ❹

Once rested pass the trig point and head for the wooden ring. Stay on the path to the left of the ring and make your way back down. This path is rocky at first. Pass over the wet sections over a couple of boardwalks.

Once you meet the forest track go right and then take the first left turn. Continue downhill ignoring a path to the left. Take the right fork to another forest track. Turn right and then left onto a small path. Veer left at the fork and put dogs back on the leads.

Once reaching the road follow back the way you came passing the house on the left and back through the entrance into the play area. Along the edge of the play area and turning left. Right at the cycle centre towards the axe man and along the path towards the car park.

16. Windermere West Easy - 7miles - 2hr 30min

This is a lovely relaxing walk which is linear, with stunning views as you walk along the waters edge of Windermere. There are grassy banks on each side of the path near the beginning of the walk with some parkland trees. There may be sheep grazing on this section. You will always be close to the water's edge and for some parts of the walk you can enjoy the shelter of the trees in hot weather as you walk through the woodlands.

How to get there - Pier 3 Car Ferry in Bowness or from Far Sawrey. Take the B5285 from Hawkshead to Far Sawrey. Once at Far Sawrey follow the signs to Windermere via the ferry. When you reach the lakeside ignore the car park on the left and continue as the road bends to the right go straight ahead over a cattle grid and the car park will be on your left a little further along the road.

Grid Reference - SD 389 955

Parking - National Trust Car Park, Pay and Display or from Bowness Ferry Car Park Pay and Display.

You will need - Dog leads, dog bags

The Walk

❶ If starting the walk from the ferry then follow the road passing the toilet block on the left. As the road bends sharply to the left, take the right turning. Follow this road now on this linear walk. If you have parked along side the lake in the National Trust car park then your walk will start here. Once out of the car park and facing the lake turn left. There are sheep grazing here and there may be traffic to the boat moorings.

Continue on this path having a couple of kissing gates to avoid cattle grids and beautiful woodlands where you continue track. It is safe to keep your dog off the out for cyclists. Walk along this path views and access to the lake in parts.

then through on the obvious lead here, but watch for some time having

You can turn around at any point on this walk but if you want to walk to Wray Castle it is roughly 3.5 miles to get there. Just follow the water's edge until you see a gate on the right, signed Wray Castle. Before going through the gate check for any grazing animals here. Once reaching Wray Castle, this is the furthest point of the walk. Retrace your steps back to your car. **❷**

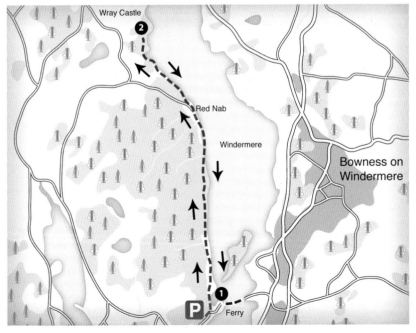

17. Claife Heights
Medium - 2.3 miles - 1hr

This walk is set as medium because of the distance, however there is a hard climb to start the walk through some beautiful woodland amongst some ancient trees. Pass a stunning building named Claife Station, built in 1790 to allow tourists to have a view of Windermere. Now currently under restoration. You will pass through some rough grassland and scrub where you will have more stunning views of Windermere. Walking alongside the lake. This walk is mostly wooded and there are lots of streams for your dog to have a drink. There is a small section of road. Sheep grazing on the last section of the walk.

How to get there - Take the B5285 from Hawkshead to Far Sawrey. Once at Far Sawrey follow the signs to Windermere via the ferry. When you reach the lakeside look out for the car park on the left before the road goes over the bridge to the ferry.

Grid Reference - Ash Landing SD389955 **Post Code** LA22 0LP

Parking - National Trust Ash Landing Car Park Pay and Display or Pier 3 Bowness Ferry Car Park pay and display.

Facilities - There are toilets at the ferry crossing.

You will need - Dog leads, dog bags

Countryside Dog Walks - Lake District - South

The Walk

1 If starting the walk from the ferry then follow the road passing the toilet block on the left. Ignore the right turn staying on the road, which will bend sharply left. Look for a second footpath on the right just after the bend in the road. Take this footpath to the car park.

From the car park take the path to the right as you face away from the lake, signed to the ferry. You can now let your dogs off the lead. Take the left turn up the steps and go straight ahead through the mixed woodlands.

Once at the top go left. Pass the Claife Station and some rocky outcrops then into deciduous woodlands with lots of ferns and mosses carpeting the forest floor. Continue to ascend the wooded hillside. The path has a series of sharp bends on your steep ascent.

Once near the plateau the paths fork left and right. **2** Take the right path signed Hawkshead. Walking along a fence line to your left and stunning views looking down to Windermere and beyond on your right. You will be pleased to know that you have reached the highest point of the walk. The path leaves the woodland behind, as you walk between bracken and open grassland. You will

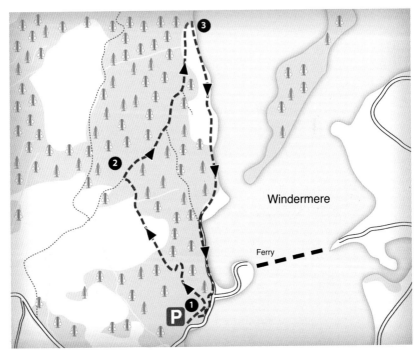

reach a stonewall to your right and a stock fence on your left. As you leave the stonewall you will cross a stream then soon pick up another stonewall on your right.

Pass through a farm gate and then turn right on a track. Through another farm gate and along the path under the canopy of trees. The path becomes rocky descending into mixed woodlands. Ignore the path on the right walking with the forest to your right and deciduous woods on the left. Ignore the stile on the right where you see the parking area and road ahead. After passing over a stream get ready to get your dog on the lead as you near the road. Once on the track go right passing through a gate to avoid the stile. Walk along the quiet access path beside the lake on your left where your dog can cool off. Take care here as cars may pass on this road, so if you can't get close control it may be better to put your dog on the lead.

❸ Go through a gate to avoid the cattle grid and continue along this path following the lakeside. Sheep may be grazing here. There are parkland trees and grassland areas. The road will narrow with fencing on both sides a little further along the road. Dogs must be on the lead here as there is access for a car park and the road is a little busier.

If you began this walk via the ferry you will see a gate on your left signed footpath to ferry just before a castle style wall to your right, which is the entrance to Claife Station. Walk through the woods and then out at the other end through another gate onto the road, turning left. You will reach the ferry on this road.

If you have parked in the car park on this side of Windermere continue ahead passing the castle style wall on your left, which is the Victorian Claife station access. Once reaching the road continue straight ahead following the road for a short while with a wall on the left and the lake over the wall. Look out for the second footpath on your right. Take this path, which will lead to the car park.

18. Brant Fell

Medium - 3.7 miles - 1hr 30min

This is a fantastic walk that has tremendous views in all directions but especially looking over Windermere. There are some roads but they are quiet leafy lanes and farm tracks. Take in the beautiful mature trees and peaceful pastures and walking a section of the Dalesway long distance path. Passing through wonderful countryside with plenty of opportunity for your dog to take a drink from the many streams and a couple of tarns. There are cattle and sheep on parts of this walk. Please note that some of the kissing gates are small so may be unsuitable for larger breeds of dog.

How to get there - From the main road out of Kendal on the A591 following for Windermere. Once in Windermere turn left at the train station onto Lake road (A5074). Turn left onto Thornbarrow Road then turning right onto Park road. Park your car before reaching the bend in the road next to the grass verge.

Grid Reference - SD 414 974

Parking - Free on the road side on the opposite side to the houses.

Facilities - There are toilets and dog friendly pubs and cafes in Windermere.

You will need - Dog leads, dog bags

The Walk

❶ From where you have parked your car continue in the same direction and look for the public footpath on the left at the bend in the road. Once on the path you can let your dog off the lead, you will pass a row of houses on your right. You will come to a gap in the stonewall with a small step. Go through this and continue straight ahead. Go through a kissing gate passing trees and through another kissing gate putting dogs back on the lead.

Go left on the track and through the small kissing gate on your left. Walk diagonally across the field and head for the next kissing gate.

Once through the kissing gate follow the sealed track and go left. Cross another sealed track and go straight ahead across the field and through a further kissing gate. Continue across the middle of a field passing through a kissing gate and again through the middle of the field passing houses to your right. Go through a kissing gate **❷** and walk between the stonewalls.

Cross a farm track ahead and continue through a gate and keep to the stonewall on your right. Through another kissing gate and turn left to follow between the stock fencing on the stoned path. You can let your dog off the lead here, as there are no grazing animals. This path starts off flat and then rises a little way. There are some nice mature trees on either side.

When the path bends sharply to the left go straight on towards the kissing gate. Go through the kissing gate putting your dog on the lead beforehand,

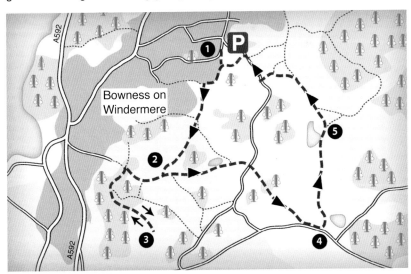

as there may be grazing animals. Go straight ahead passing some mature Oak trees and once at the top of the hill you will be met with fantastic views over Windermere.

Go over the rocky outcrop behind the bench and follow the path towards another kissing gate. There may be cattle grazing here. Once through the kissing gate take this permissive path towards the rocky outcrop ahead on the obvious worn grassy path. Once reaching the top of the rocks the views are magnificent on a clear day. ❸

Once you have taken in the views go back the way you came down towards the kissing gate. Once through the kissing gate follow the grassy track back to the bench and right back through the kissing gate and left. Dogs back off the lead here. Keep on this path until you are back at the two kissing gates by the stonewall.

Put your dogs back on the lead and go right through the kissing gate and follow the Dalesway long distance footpath. Keep on the stoned path with the stonewall on the left. There are stunning mature oaks and parkland trees. Ignore the steps right and pass through another gate where you can let your dogs off the lead again. Walking between the stonewalls and crossing a farm track ahead and continue straight on.

Pass through another small kissing gate where you will need your dog on the lead again as you go into the field. Keep to the stonewall on your right and continue ahead. Go through a kissing gate and follow the obvious path diagonally across the field. There may be cattle grazing here but they should be well used to people, as this is a widely used path.

Pass through a lovely iron gate, which is weighted to ensure that it closes. Keep to the iron fence on the right, which leads to an access road. At the road go right then almost immediately left and through a kissing gate.

Once through the kissing gate let your dogs off the leads and pass an avenue of mature beech trees and a woodland copse to your right and a mire to your left where you can rest a while on the bench and let your dog cool off in the water.

Continue on and through a further kissing gate passing pine trees then through another kissing gate to cross a farm road and through another kissing gate. Walk between the fences passing a stable block and house on the other side to your right.

Put dogs on the leads again then go through another kissing gate, cross the road and through another kissing gate. Pass trees on your right and veer right

to follow the fence line on the left with hilly rocky outcrops to your right. Look for the directional finger post. You will find water just before going through another kissing gate.

Through the wood pasture walking straight ahead following the finger posts then another kissing gate passing an oak tree then through another kissing gate passing a copse of trees then another kissing gate keeping to the stone wall to your left.

Ascend the hill and through a gate then right on a sealed access road, which is quiet and beautifully wooded. Keep your dogs on leads here, as there is a busy road ahead. ❹ Once at the road go left and then immediately left. Walk between fence and wall but keeping dogs on leads as the road on the right is busy and there are gaps in the wall.

Once reaching the end of the path go back onto the road and immediately left onto a quiet access road. Pass a lake on the right. Pass several driveways then through a kissing gate and along a stoned path across fields. Through a farm gate where you can let your dogs off the leads. Walking between stock fencing with trees either side.

Dogs on leads again as you go through a gate passing a mere on the left. Through a further gate walking between a fence and stonewall which open out into grazed fields. Your dog will find water on the left when reaching a stream. Lots of gorse and scrub here. Ignore the footpath that goes to the right and back but keep straight on. ❺ You have now left the Dalesway long distance path.

Cross a stream via stepping-stones and through a gate. When reaching two paths take the left fork. Pass through this rocky scrubby field on the obvious path. Go through a kissing gate and then left on this access road.

Once reaching a quiet road go right for a short distance looking out for a footpath on the left. Pass through a kissing gate into a field heading towards a house. Pass the houses and through another kissing gate. It is safe to let your dogs off the leads here. Continue along a fence passing trees. The path bends sharply and goes back on itself. Once reaching another path put your dog on the lead and go right at the backs of houses to the road and back to your car.

19. High Dam

Medium - 1.8 miles - 45min

This stunning walk is a real treat for you and your dog, with water all the way and walking through some stunning woodland with ferns and mosses carpeting the floor and rocky boulders giving real atmosphere. As you leave the woodland and enter the forest you will be met with two glorious reservoirs crossing wooden bridges and following the water through the forest with some mixed woodlands and a little heathland.

How to get there - On the A590 out of Newby Bridge following for Barrow and Ulverston then cross a road bridge over the river following signs for Hawkshead. As you pass the Swan Inn take the road on the left following the river. Once reaching a junction go right heading for Finsthwaite. Once passing a large farm yard on the left and a few more houses High Dam car park will be found on a left turn. If you come to further road signs for Hawkshead and Ferry you have just passed it.

Grid Reference - SD 367 882
Post Code - LA12 8NB

Parking - Pay and display

Facilities - There are no facilities

You will need - Lead for car park

The Walk

1 From the car park take the path next to the river, which ascends into the woods, just after the pay and display. Once on your ascent you will see a path to the left that goes parallel to the river.

Ignore the footbridge on the left and veer right, walking up the rocky path. The woodland is predominantly Oaks. Stay on the path and once you have passed the rocky outcrop the path bends to the left to continues running parallel with the river. Follow this path.

Keep to the main path ascending the woodlands. Pass through a kissing gate and follow straight on ignoring the right turn. The woodland becomes forest here having more coniferous trees.

Stay on the path with the dam to your left. Cross a couple of footbridges where you then reach a second dam. **2** Cross the footbridge on the right and continue following the path as it follows near to the water's edge.

Ignore a kissing gate ahead but stay on the path with the stonewall to your right. Pass through a gap where the stonewalls meet. Continue on the path, which can get wet under foot. The path ascends again through the woods, which are now dominated by silver birch.

Pass over a footbridge and continue straight on following on the path above the water. The vegetation changes here to bracken, heather and bilberry. The woodlands change to conifers once more. Pass through a gap in the stonewall, then left over another footbridge.

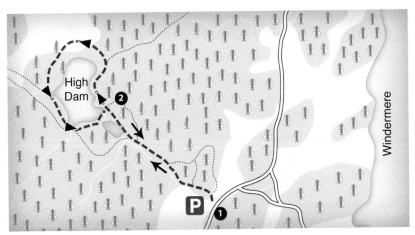

You are back near the water's edge where your dog can enjoy a cool drink. Continue on the path back into the woodlands crossing another footbridge where you continue straight on.

Cross the dam wall and take the path before the bridge to the right to continue on the path of which you came. Downhill now all the way back to your car.

20. Gummer's How

Medium - 1.2 miles - 45min

This is a short walk, which inclines steadily for most of the first half. The incline isn't hard going and the views are truly amazing looking over Windermere on the way up and at the top so wait for a clear day. There is water along the way for your dog with some trees and beautiful heathland amongst rocky crags. There may be cattle grazing for conservation purposes, but a gentle breed being Highland x Beef short horns, see page four for more advice on cattle.

How to get there - Follow the A590 to Newby Bridge then take the A592 signed Bowness and Windermere. Take the road on the right, signed Gummer's How and Cartmel Fell and Bowland Bridge. The Forestry Commission car park will be on your right a little further along this road.

Grid Reference - SD 389876

Parking - Free in car park

Facilities - There are no facilities on this walk

You will need - Leads

The Walk

❶ From the car park head away from the road and take the footpath on the left towards the end of the car park. There is a stream here where your dogs can get a drink. Ascend into the forest for a short while. At the kissing gate put your dog on the lead.

Cross the quiet road and back through a small gate. **❷** Keep dogs under close control as there may be cattle here. Continue ahead following the path. There are views of lake Windermere on your left.

Pass through some conifers, which then becomes woodland copse of mainly Silver birch. Cross over a stream that runs under the path where your dog can get a drink. Climb the steps and rocky areas. You will see a fence line on your right half way up the steps. At the corner of this fence line you can either choose to take the path on the right (option a) or continue straight on where you will have a couple of small boulders to climb (option b).

Option A.

Turn right at the corner of the fence line and follow this path, which will bend to the left passing some larch trees then turn right. The area here has some beautiful heathland again up a small hill and pass a rocky boulder under foot. Walk straight on through more trees and left on the obvious path. Here it is open with rocky boulders and heathland. Look straight ahead for the trig point and stop here a while for amazing views of Windermere. If you are lucky the heather will be in flower. You can then when you are ready turn back the way you came for an easy descent back down.

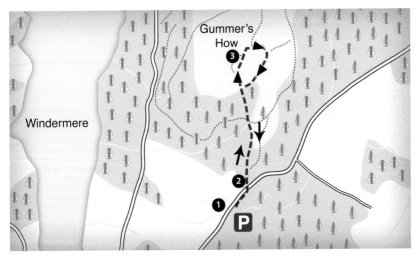

Option B.

Continue straight ahead passing over some rocky outcrops then ascending the stone steps. A little climb over rock will bring you onto higher ground where the views are truly outstanding.

Head for the trig point and if you are lucky the heather will be in flower, which adds to the beauty.
❸ Pass the trig point and take the path descending in the opposite direction moving away from the lake view. This path turns back on itself and you will be heading back in the direction that you came.

Look for the path going left amongst the trees, which is way marked. Once you reach the corner of the fence line again turn left and continue back down on this path, and back to your car.

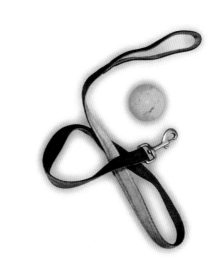